D0841323

FISH BONES AND

Bread Crumbs

A Guided Journal

BURGUNDI ALLISON

© Burgundi Allison

Print ISBN: 978-1-54398-703-4

eBook ISBN: 978-1-54398-704-1

PREFACE
Save the Scraps

In 2012 Jesus revealed Himself to me as Lord and prompted me to write a blog to chronicle His works and redeem that time.

TD Jakes preached a sermon titled 'Save the Scraps.' The text was Mark 6:42-52, the miracle of the 5 thousand fed, but the focus was verses 43 and 52- the taking of the scraps and their significance. Bishop Jakes began with this statement – "That which remains is greater than that which was lost." He highlights verse 41 where Jesus blesses the five loaves and two fish, admonishing that He is blessing what is not enough; and that the blessing and multiplication happens at the breaking. Selah.

He goes on to discuss how he pondered why they load the twelve baskets of fragments on to the boat (v43). As the account goes, Jesus goes up to pray and the disciples face a storm in the middle of the night, which Jesus can see, and after a while, He walks out onto the water toward them. They are afraid, assuming He is a ghost; He quiets their fears and gets into the boat with them and the winds cease. Verses 51 and 52 detail how amazed the disciples are because they had not understood the loaves.

The Bishop preaches that God intended the overflow at the feeding of the 5,000 precisely for the disciples to take the fragments with them in the boat. He goes on to say that the storm they faced was designed to test them. The scraps from the feeding of the 5,000 were in the boat to be a reminder to them of God's miraculous works past, that they would not fear the present danger. Jesus was concerned with their mentality, their way of thinking; He wanted them to see Him in the scraps, to remember His signs and wonders and be bold and unafraid going forward.

The blog that would become this journal is my ode to my scraps. His directive to get it out, was to preserve it, so I would not forget what He's done and how He's done it so that I would be not afraid, or doubtful, or worrisome moving forward. And most importantly, that I would use my scraps to build a platform to feed another growing woman.

INTRODUCTION

I n the second chapter of Genesis, God, in verse 18 decides that *"It is not good that man should be alone; I will make him a helper comparable to him."* Skip to verse 22 and voila- *"Then the rib which the Lord God had taken from the man He made into a woman, and he brought her to the man."*

My first read of the making of Eve left me awestruck. Women have been bred and led to believe that man, in all ways, is superior to woman. That he was created to rule over us because of his inherent superiority; but right there in Genesis 2:18, it is written- *helper.* Never mind that the immediate next word is comparable, I was struck by the use of the word *helper.* Who gets help from someone who is less than capable? Less than able? Weaker? Ill equipped? My point here is that God knew that man is less than perfectly capable. Less than able. Not as strong. Not fully equipped; And in His infinite wisdom, created for him a *helper.*

The creation of Eve is the culmination of the creation story. There is no mention, at creation, of what Adam is to her, except that he is to leave his family to join *to* her (v 24) because she is *"bone of my bones and flesh of my flesh...because she*

3

was taken out of me." This foreshadows the command of Eph 5:28 *"So husbands ought to love their wives as their own bodies; he who loves his wife loves himself."* As God reveals Himself as the initiator of the bond between man and woman, the roles designed for them in the relationship are also revealed. Eve was formed out of her husband not to be subservient to him but to serve him. In serving him, she was pleasing God. Go back to verse 18- God says, *"it is NOT good that man be alone..."* Eve was created not to please Adam, but to please God. Adam was none the wiser that help was necessary, until God brought her to him.

Isn't that just like God? To know something about you that you don't know about yourself. To know what you need when you don't even know you need it? I have heard it said that a man doesn't know who he is until he knows what kind of woman he wants. And if you are a man after God's heart, the woman you want is the woman God brings to you, so your manhood is hinged on your God sent helper. This is how a man is made perfectly capable. Perfectly able. Strong. Equipped; by submitting his desires to the authority of the God who created him and allowing this same God to lead him to the helper He created for him.

Helpers- please recognize that God created you with capabilities, abilities, strength and equipment to join to the man he created you for. These elements are God given, and so they must be God tested, God tried, God proven. If you submit yourself to His will, not only in seeking relationship with a man, but in seeking to be a woman of God, He will isolate you: He wants you for

Himself. Verse 21 says ***"the Lord God caused a deep sleep to fall on Adam, and he slept; and He took one of his ribs and closed up the flesh in its place..."*** Adam was in a God-induced coma while the Lord made Eve. In her making, there was just the woman and her Lord.

The work of becoming is singular.

How this book works

You pray.

You read.

You reflect.

You pray.

I prompt.

You reflect.

You write.

You pause. Wherever necessary. As often as necessary.

Let's get started

There are those that boast in not having a counterpart to answer to or consider and there are the others- forlorn and longing for the 'one.' I believe that these extremes run deep and counter to the process of being single.

Being single has been revealed to me as a process in which a woman learns who she is, who God is, His love for her and her love for herself. It is a time of healing, preparation, testing, solitude, reflection, learning. Notice that I did not use the term season as it connotes an end; and while there are women who mark the end of this process at the point of marriage, I offer in these pages that the destination is wholeness.

I have a heart for single women; a heart that is often pained at our inability to learn the lessons presented to us during this delicate time in our lives. There are lessons that we learn in relationships as young women that should inform the relationship decisions we make as we get older- and yet, so many of us repeat those young lady mistakes as growing women.

The biggest point I missed, is that when you stagnate your growth, you enable growing men to remain youthful. Youth is reserved for fools- foolish ideals, foolish acts and behaviors, the shirking of responsibility, fear of commitment- we help breed this in men when we deny the wisdom of our experiences.

Women love to chant about self-love, but you can't love who you don't know. And if you consistently reject the grace of the lessons, you dishonor yourself. And there is no love where there is dishonor. And he sees this. It's part of the reason he chose you. It is *the* reason you have not changed your decision to be with him.

I have been called to assist in making your process fruitful. I will give it to you straight- no chaser- but if you submit to your truth, and the pain, it'll all go down smooth...

SECTION 1-
GET NEKKID

Reflection 1

Gen 2:21-25

But for Adam no suitable helper was found. 21 So the Lord God caused the man to fall into a deep sleep; and while he was sleeping, he took one of the man's ribs and then closed up the place with flesh. 22 Then the Lord God made a woman from the rib he had taken out of the man, and he brought her to the man.

23 The man said,

"This is now bone of my bones and flesh of my flesh; she shall be called 'woman,' for she was taken out of man."

25 Adam and his wife were both naked, and they felt no shame.

Genesis 3: 6 When the woman saw that the fruit of the tree was good for food and pleasing to the eye, and also desirable for gaining wisdom, she took some and ate it. She also gave some to her husband, who was with her, and he ate it. 7 Then the eyes of both of them were opened, and they realized they were naked; so, they sewed fig leaves together and made coverings for themselves.

As you read the scriptures above, you must note the tranquility between them while they were naked under God. The desire for things outside of His expressed will is what upset the atmosphere. Isn't that what upsets our homes and relationships? Wanting things outside of the goodness He has already given; hiding from ourselves and each other as we seek those things outside of the parameters He's set. Trying, in vain, to cover what is plain- that we are flawed. That we make mistakes.

I struggle with intimacy. No issues taking my clothes off- but major hindrances to emotional nudity. Vulnerability is not my strong suit. This is precisely why it has been so easy for me to walk away from any relationship that necessitated my vulnerability, and ultimately why I've never known the kind of love that I desire. It literally pains me to allow a person to see me in pain. If you hurt me, and I show you, I feel like I'm extracting the bullet from my wound and handing it over saying "thank you sir, may I have another?"

I won't give you tears. I won't give you a story to tell. You cannot have my heart to add to the collection in your jar. So, as I cry silently to myself about how no one wants my heart, I must come to the place where I realize that I haven't offered it.

Why not?

Because I know too much. I've learned by way of man- mother, father, high school and college boyfriends, girlfriends, aunts, uncles and grandparents, tv and music- to be ashamed of my weaknesses. (***Gen 3:7***) I've learned that relationships are games people play and the goal is to not get hurt. I've learned that at each level, as the stakes get higher, to cover myself even more. That playing fair gets you nowhere and to protect my heart at the cost of sharing it. I've learned that to be vulnerable with a man is to leave yourself open for him to do what men do- whatever the hell they want at your expense, and so to never be that open. To never be that vulnerable.

What I am discovering, is that to know partnership in the ways God intended is to return to the shameless nakedness of First Man and First Woman. When you open yourself to Him, He will send the people that will exhort you, create the circumstances that will stun you, and nurse the wounds that you will undress. And when you can look at yourself bare, and unashamed, you are seeing what God sees- that is the beginning of unconditional love. That is the true invitation for Him to be at the Center of your life, and any relationship you create thereafter. Selah.

Go Deeper
Read Genesis 2 in its entirety, focusing on Adam and Eve's nakedness.

1. **How do you define naked in this sense?**

2. How do you receive the concept of being naked without shame?

3. What was the thing- experience, person- that first invited shame into your life, making you cover yourself?

Reflection 2

Is 43:18,19

'Forget the former things; do not dwell on the past. See, I am doing a new thing! Now it springs up; do you not perceive it? I am making a way in the wilderness and streams in the wasteland."

Our first experience with love is with our parent(s), and everything we learn being loved by them, loving them, and watching them love, become the primary influences on how and who we love. But, can we love through life blaming our parents' relationship issues for our failures? And do they reap the benefits of praise when we get it right?

Hell, to the NO! Yes, your parents are charged with setting the foundation for your ability to love, and, yes, they are also responsible for the development of your self -esteem, but the manifestation of *how* you love and *who* you become- in life and in relationships- is up to you. Pointing blame at them shirks your responsibility to learn.

Likewise, mom's and dad's harmonious union is not a sure bet that that lightening will strike twice- the onus remains on you to learn the lessons of their trials and triumphs and apply them appropriately.

There is a difference between credit due and credit earned; their deeds are done, what will you do with the wisdom that remains? Selah.

Go Deeper

1. **What did you learn about love from your parents? Consider also their absence if applicable, and how it shaped your ideals of love.**

2. **What did you learn about your role as a woman in a relationship watching your mother navigate hers?**

3. **How does your mother show up in you in your own relationships? Consider also the things you do in deliberate opposition to what you saw her do.**

Reflection 3

My first love started out as a great friend (isn't that what we're taught? That great loves begin as great friends?). We were teenagers, just hanging, until the day he asked me out. He was a few years older than me and I loved him! And as teenaged girls do, I planned my life around him, being his wife and having his babies. He had this habit of spending too much time with his friends; ditching me to be with them. They were ignorant teenaged boys and I grew to hate them, out of resentment that he preferred being with them over being with me. We didn't hang out anymore, I was his girlfriend now, so we went on dates, and no matter how much fun we had, it was a date and with that came some responsibility for entertaining me that drained him and drove him away from me and to his ignorant friends.

Vying for his attention, as I thought I had to, I became a lil'teenaged beyotch. I nagged, complained, became almost unbearable to be around- too laborious to be fun for a teenaged boy. But this was serious business for me, as it is for too many teenaged girls. The relationship became too much for him and he set his sights on someone else. He was honest, telling me straight up that he wanted to explore this other option- a girl a few years younger than me who also attended our school. #humiliated

Somewhere along the way there was another lil'miss somebody who tickled his fancy and he tried his hand with her, too. I was hurt and embarrassed, our school was small, so everyone knew that while I pined over him, he was doing what boys do. Eventually, he decided to just call the whole thing off- offering that as he was leaving for college, it was not in his best interest to be tied down in a relationship. Ok. Even then, I had enough of a mind to not chase. I let him go.

He left for school, without seeing me, just a goodbye phone call. I set about the business of getting over him. I had an inkling that I was good; that regardless of where a boy could go, or what girl he'd come across, there would be none like me.

He called me, maybe a quarter of the way into his first semester to tell me that in all of Atlanta, "Black Man's Paradise" as he called it, there was not a girl with a face as beautiful as mine. Ya think? He wanted me. And went through all the motions to get me- mixtapes ('member them?), cards, flowers, serenades, a ring- sapphires and diamonds and matching bracelet- but I was unmoved. My mother told me to let my head rule my heart, and I learned, quickly, how to. I gave him hell. I was cold and distant. Sometimes downright mean while he wooed me and exposed his emotions to me. Payback is a 16-year-old bitch. I bled him until he walked away- hurt.

I learned from him you cannot depend on someone else to bear the responsibility of making you happy. I came to understand that you cannot keep a boy (man) that does not want to be kept, and that if he can walk away from you- let him. I know from this relationship that there is no love like my love, and the best way to prove that to a man is to give him the opportunity to find out. I also learned that a broken heart is not sudden death. He is responsible for my reverence for honesty above all else in a relationship. And I grew capable of bearing that kind of honesty, demanding it even.

Some of us have allowed ourselves to believe that our first loves were inconsequential, that they lacked substance and are irrelevant to who and how we love today. Believe that and you probably believe that you're ready for love- to receive and reciprocate- right now. Selah.

Go Deeper

1. **What did you learn about how men love from your father? - this applies to lessons learned in his absence.**

2. **How can you now see how your father shows up in your relationships?**

3. **What did you learn about yourself from your first love?**

4. **In what ways (if at all) has your first love shown up in your relationships?**

Reflection 4

My best friend is one of the most difficult people I know. Her choice of words and their patterns are often misunderstood. Her behavior taken as strange. Her demeanor mistaken as mean or crazy. I have often been called on to translate for others what exactly it is that she is trying to say, or to give meaning to awkward 'acting out.'

When we were younger, we were 'asshole' tight. If we were not together, there was a reason, and one knew exactly where the other could be found. As we've grown, there has emerged a divide between us. We have friends outside of the circle that forged around us. We live apart. Our lives have taken turns away from one another. But she remains my best friend. She knows me better than anyone else, even myself at times. She knows my heart and can speak to its issues. We have a rhythm- we can feel a disagreement or argument mounting and know when it's time to separate or shut up. We don't talk everyday anymore, but when there is a need, that same urgency- that drop everything because she needs me- is still there. Amongst our other friends, mutual and otherwise, it is common knowledge that though she may spend more time with so-and-so, or I may talk more often with such-and-such, I am her best friend, and she is mine. Everyone knows that. We make sure that everyone knows that.

Our relationship ebbs and flows now, after 16 years. We have waves of intensity where we do talk every day and we spend more time together than usual. Where we laugh uncontrollably at nothing at all and absolutely everything. And those times pass. And we only talk casually, and we spend most of our time with our other friends. But there is no love lost. And neither of us is under the impression that anything has changed, we have accepted the maturation of our relationship. And our relationship has taken work. Not the kind that you are aware of, it has not been dogged. But the kind of work that you do for a worthwhile cause. We weren't looking for each other when we crossed paths, but here we are. And neither of us had to stand by, with, for, the other in those times when we have. But we did.

At times being 'us' has taken a lot out of me, but I'm sure that who 'I' am would be very different if not for her. But as I look back over our relationship, what confounds me is how effortless it seems. The concessions made, the compromises, the things not said in wisdom, the ebb and flow- none of it was thought about or calculated- it was just done. It was done because it was what the relationship required to stay alive. Not unchanged, but alive.

This is all very poignant to me now as I examine what it is I really want out of a relationship. My best friend is the longest and most complex relationship I've had, and so I am using it as my template. Not that my man should replace my best friend, but that my relationship with a man should fall together as freely, and the effort to keep it together should flow as naturally. Because, as I have realized is true about my best friend, on some level I will need him, and the urgency of him as a necessary part of my life should drive the concessions, compromises, and things not said in wisdom, straight through whatever fears, doubts or pride that would threaten our relationship.

I want to be in a relationship with a man where I am secure enough to allow it to ebb and flow. I am not good with the cooling down of a hot beginning. It has always signaled 'the end,' to me. Looking at my best friendship what I see is how paramount having a life outside of each other is to avoid the stranglehold. More importantly, I am learning to appreciate what it says about a relationship that it can ebb, and flow. It speaks about its strength. That no matter where I go or how far- I know, you know, and everybody else knows- exactly where and to whom we will return.

I want a relationship minus the angst and anxiety. I want the work to feel like breathing- deceptively simple. Selah.

Go Deeper

1. **What qualities does your bff have that make you feel safe?**

2. **Which of these qualities are necessary for you to extend to yourself for you to feel safe in your own skin?**

3. **Are these same qualities ones that you require in a man? Why or why not?**

SECTION 2- THE WOMAN GOD IS MAKING

Reflection 1

read 1 Corinthians 7:32-35

I have great revelations near water. When I need to be near God, to hear Him most clearly, feel Him most intimately, I go to water. At home, I jump in the shower. And the beach serves as my ultimate 'upper room.' At the kitchen sink, washing dishes, I have visions. Brushing my teeth with the water running (don't judge me), I think with great clarity. It is the water that clears my mind allowing me to receive. In the shower a few days ago I asked the Lord a question; considering that one of my best friends was on the path to her second marriage while I had not been graced with a first, I asked – "why not me?" Not in a 'woe is me' vain, but seeking a factual, logical answer for why it is that love, and committed relationships, marriage, seem to fall into the laps of some while remaining fleeting and elusive for others. And I wanted an answer.

Cut to no more than three steps from the shower- me at the sink brushing my teeth. Same morning, and voila! He answers:

Genesis 2:18- "it is not good for the man to be alone. I will make a helper suitable for him."

I Corinthians 7:34- "an unmarried woman is concerned about the Lord's affairs. Her aim is to be devoted to the Lord in both body and spirit. But a married woman is concerned about the affairs of this world- how she can please her husband."

Psalm 37:4- "take delight in the Lord and He will give you the desire of your heart."

There is no promise of a husband for any woman. Genesis 3:16 tells us that all that is promised between man and woman is strife- **"your desire will be for your husband and he will rule over you."** The conflict being the woman's desire for a man against whom she is powerless.

There are some women for whom God provides by way of a husband. Her needs are met through the provision of a man. He is the manifestation of God's love, protection, provision for her. There are women for whom their make is tethered to a man. It is their nature to nurture and help him and God provides a man's suitable helper through her. But this is not every woman. This is certainly not me, naturally.

An unmarried woman is to be consumed with the things of God. I surmise that this is the time in which a woman becomes a Godly woman. When she grows in relationship with God to approach intimacy with the Lord. It is when she learns His heart for her and develops a heart for Him. It is both endearing and sometimes unpleasant. It is proving to be the most vulnerable I have ever been. I am aware of an omnipresent God from whom I cannot hide my fears, my insecurities, the wants of my flesh, my displeasures, my anger, my pride. I am fully naked. And for every layer exposed, there is a challenge to deal with the skin shed. I cannot sweep it away. I must run the shavings through my fingers- feel the texture against the open flesh and bits of skin growing to replace it. I must cry over it and mourn it and celebrate it. And the skin is the largest of the body's organs: this shit could take forever!

My husband is not a need. He is my heart's deepest desire. The one God knew to touch, slightly enough to awaken, deep enough that I would yield, gentle not to make me bleed. He told me, almost four years ago now, that He wanted me to Himself. This I got at my kitchen sink doing dishes. I cried so hard I shook. The thought that He wanted me to Himself. It was sweet, then. Still is. But it is hard. And no one 'gets' it. That's how I know I'm doing it right. I am a Godly woman and He is a jealous God. He'll give me up when He's ready. I am finding the delight in that.

Go Deeper

1.   **Have you found the joy in being single? Describe your single joy-**

2. **What parts of being single hurt?**

3. **How do you encourage yourself during the difficult moments?**

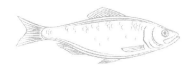

Reflection 2

Doors. It is a recurring theme in my life right now, and today in particular, the word itself has appeared in my reading, studying, and work. I am studying The Book of Revelations and in the 6th letter of the 7 letters to the 7 churches, to Philadelphia John is instructed to write ***"I know your works. See, I have set before you an open door, and no one can shut it; for you have a little strength, have kept my Word, and have not denied My name."***

This passage recalled a vision I've had of swinging doors, a symbol of relationships as God would have them. When He opens the door, you cannot shut it because your strength is limited. An effort to shut it is futile, it will swing; always giving to re-entry. And this is what he wants from me. To be unhinged. To extend to myself the same grace that covers me.

Expectant mothers read books, talk to other moms, their moms, doctors, about what to expect while carrying and what it will be like once the baby has arrived. Her body is daily preparing for delivery and as her baby grows and her body changes, she must constantly adjust her way of doing things to accommodate what **is**, but hasn't come, yet. This is demonstrative of our evolution from the woman man made to the woman God made.

You are the woman that your experiences have made you. Your journey with God is the walk to unlearn you, know Him, and discover the woman He created you to be. She is the spirit that gets convicted when you know what you know but do otherwise. She is the best of you. She is who hears Him when He speaks-the first time; she hears the slightest whisper. She is already within you, dwelling with His spirit. This walk is about birthing her. And a true connection with God.

Like labor, it will take an unknown amount of time and yours will be different than every other woman (although that will not keep other women from telling you how to do this). Add space for mishaps and missteps and mistakes. This is not about perfecting you, it is about perfecting the faith that will change you. It is about learning through the mishaps, missteps and mistakes that God does not demand perfection. He demands perseverance.

You are pregnant. And every day God is preparing you for what **is**, but hasn't come, yet. You must learn to let the door swing and that it swings both ways- as certainly as you can walk out, you can walk back in. All the coming and going is strengthening your discernment, your resolve, your reliance on Him. The same reliance, resolve, and discernment that are necessary for any relationship.

Go Deeper

1. **What things do you hold against yourself?**

2. **How will you be more gracious to yourself?**

Reflection 3

read Ecclesiastes 3:1-8, 11, 15

In the book of Ecclesiastes, we are told that *'to everything there is a season, a time for every purpose under heaven:'* and the Lord goes on to illustrate ways in which those seasons and purposes play out in our lives.

Spring is lauded as a time of renewal. It is the season celebrated for breakthrough. The first signs of spring are the sure signs that winter is coming to an end. I hate winter. It is cold. Often it is gray. Most times, it feels the most prolonged of the seasons. It is the time when most of us spend the most time alone. For some, it is a time where you are most vulnerable to depression and angst. It is dark early, making dark seem long. And we complain, "it's too cold."

In our lives, our faith is built, shaken, tested and proven by the seasons of Ecclesiastes. How mightily clever of our God to pattern the spiritual growth of His creation by the physical manifestation of change in the earth He formed, and I want us to be mindful of how God uses the seasons to reveal to us His truth.

If you take a moment, and examine where you are, right now, on this leg of your journey, you will notice that you are in a place, feeling a feeling, doing a thing that you have done, felt and been before. And if you look further, you will notice that although you have altered facets of you *this* time, you have probably given yourself way too much credit for how different you are doing things, this time. If you dare to go even deeper, if you chart your course from where you are right now, you will see that should you stay on the path that you are on, you will end up right where you ended the last time you were in this place, feeling this feeling, doing these same things.

A cycle is usually represented as a circle, connoting that it cannot be undone; but within a cycle there is an embedded a process in which elements are divided out and a phase ends, allowing the remaining elements to fuse together and the cycle to continue. This process occurs repeatedly, regenerating constantly by means of the same sequence. God has brought us to places familiar. He has divided past things to end old phases and led us to new experiences with which we must fuse to continue. He has divided it, but have you given it up?

"That which is has already been, and what is to be has already been; And God requires an account of what is past." Ecclesiastes 3:15 Our pasts are significant for our present. God orchestrated cycles for all of the life that He created with an expressed purpose that the past be accounted for, but as all things work for the good of those who love Him and are called according to His purpose, His grace will allow for our pasts to account for our elevation.

Go Deeper

1. **What devastating event from your past with time proved to work for your good?**

2. How is this thing tied to your purpose?

SECTION 3-
FIGHTING FOR HER

Reflection 1

I had a moment this morning. I was fighting mad but was reminded that I was fighting wrong. God, I love you! I love how you can read my mind and know my heart and give a word at the right time. To correct. To encourage. To exhort. To sustain. This morning's word was a call to arms. He reminded me that in this battle, I had chosen the wrong weapons. I was using my tongue to cut. The tongue that harms and can kill. The one that can halt enemy fire by breaking the human host's spirit. 'No,' He said. Words like salt, heap, coals came to mind. My mind was flooded with scripture admonishing me to see the unseen, battle not the flesh. And I began to pray. Asking that my Lord give me discernment to know what I am up against and the wisdom to choose my weapons accordingly. I thanked Him, for having brought me to this very place, against this familiar enemy before. Once I did not have the wisdom that comes by knowledge of His word and did not know how to fight. I thanked Him because in this round, I took captive my thoughts and submitted them to Him, and He gave me a battle plan. I thanked Him because I know His plan, and it is not to hurt me, nor that I should be defeated.

I am marked. For Christ. I come out of one thing, and another rears its head. These 'things' are personal. Meant to sift out that which is not conducive to a Christ-like me. Meant to test my commitment and resolve to His commands. Meant to enlarge my territory. Meant to heighten and condition my senses. Meant for my good.

So, I take deep breaths, and keep fighting. From glory to glory.

Go Deeper

1. **What is your natural weapon of choice, i.e., - words, hands- and how is God dealing with you concerning your weapon?**

2. **In what ways are you holding onto the things God is telling you to put down in order to be in stronger relationship with Him?**

3. **How often are you challenged in this area?**

_____

_____

_____

_____

_____

_____

_____

_____

_____

_____

_____

_____

_____

_____

_____

_____

_____

_____

_____

_____

_____

_____

_____

_____

222

Reflection 2

I like sex. But I am choosing to follow the Spirit and lock up my virtue- from myself and others. This is my thing- the sin that so easily ensnares. Not because I so enjoy the act of sex, but more so because I can. Because I am a woman, the odds are stacked in my favor that I will score more often than a man. And smart women know, you can cripple a man with sex. Make him soft. Weak. Dumb. Gullible. And I learned very early that men can do the same to women, so, I sought out to do, rather than be done.

It is important to join your head and your heart, but there is an additional step- severing your sex from your heart and joining your sex to your head. Got it? Men can manipulate a woman's emotions using sex when a woman uses her heart as a sex organ. She gets caught up in how he makes her "feel" when they have sex, and the "feeling" lingers after the act (which, had she been using her head, she would know that that feeling is actually a chemical reaction, having nothing to do with emotional connect-edness).

These women have no mind, because it is being ruled by their heart, which is being used in the act of sex, thereby saturating it with endorphins secreted by a man that is solely in control of his mental, emotional and sexual faculties. Miss Kitty- we have a problem!

But, alas, there are also problems that arise for those of us who do successfully extract our hearts from our loins- we become uber efficient at choosing partners for the sole purpose of temporal pleasure, and as time passes we realize that in order to have what we really want (love), we will have to unlearn the rules the world created to become who we were created to be.

I was reminded by my Godfather that "*a virtuous woman is molded and formed by the Spirit.*"

Who we are prior to submitting ourselves to God, is the makeup of the outcomes of every relationship we've had prior- with dad, boyfriends, girlfriends, one-night stands, hookups, and the like. Whatever mode of thinking, whatever type of being you employed to move through your life the way you did before you gave it to Him, must be undone. Part of my undoing is in my sex.

Through study and alone time with God I have learned that it was not His intention that I compartmentalize my sexuality. Instead what He wanted from me was that I change my mind and fix it on Him, allowing Him to turn my heart to flesh and learn love His way. That way, my heart and mind are joined and my sex falls under the commands of His word, rather than the game.

Not easy.

But my desires have also changed, which makes it a little easier. I am sensitive to the indwelling Holy Spirit and try to be careful not to grieve it. I am not dating because my flesh is weak. A date is cool, but to date one person will undoubtedly tempt my appetite, and, yea...

Call me conceited, but this celibacy thing makes me feel sexier than I did was I was in the game. I feel like I'm holding the center of the universe between my thighs and how many men dare go there?

Exactly!

Go Deeper

1. **How do you manage your sexuality?**

2. **How have you submitted your sexuality to God?**

Reflection 3

I have been waiting- to be inspired on my job, to know what happens next, to get to next- and as I do in most things, I started out hungry- for God, His word, His wisdom, the desires of His heart for me- but as I yielded control to Him, in me grew the familiar disdain for being out of control, and with that began to settle the discontent of not knowing, not moving, and ultimately a misery for the wait.

I've studied waiting, scripturally. Patience is not a virtue that I inherently possess, and I have been aware that what He wants from me are the things I cannot do, will not do, willingly, and so this patience bit has been a thorn in my side. What I have learned in my studies is that waiting is not passive. It is an active form of worship where we acknowledge God- His infinite wisdom, power and love.

When He benches you, the highest form of worship is waiting with an expectant heart, a grateful heart, a humble heart, a thirsty heart and open yourself to receive His wisdom.

Sounds good. Feels difficult.

I lost focus. I was increasing, leaving less and less room for the Spirit to lead me, so I began seeing things through my own eyes and began to dislike the way things looked. Deserted. Immobile. Real effed up.

And then this friend of mine told me, in a nutshell, that I was waiting wrong. And I remembered. And began to appreciate the time I've been given to work some things out.

Waiting is a time of preparation and with correction I was able to see how God was using the time to mold me and to reveal Himself more fully to me. I was waiting for the time to pass, totally missing that this time is a gift. Selah.

Go Deeper
1. **What are you waiting for?**

2. **Have you learned to appreciate your wait, or do you resent it?**

3. **If you resent it, what will you do to redeem the time?**

Reflection 4

An old love came to see me. I had been dreaming of him. The first few were all set in bedrooms. I was always uncomfortable, covering myself and he was making some statement regarding getting me, or having me. As the dreams progressed, I became more vocal, asking him to leave, and finally telling him to get out of my bedroom. He became more aggressive in each one, finally appearing almost naked until I tossed him some clothes and ordered him out. I noticed that a dream always preceded him showing up.

I am taken aback when he offers to buy me lunch. Not by the offer, but at his presence. I was certain that it was done. That whatever he was looking for that necessitated his reach for me in the first place, he'd found and was able to move on. But our same friend, in the waking world, is confident that he has not moved on. Before he reappeared, she gave me warning that he would show up again. "NO. It's done, I rebuke you for that!" She laughed. Another friend shared the same thought, taking a grim step further inferring that it would be different when he returned, and that I should be cautious. Pissed seems about right. I felt so accomplished walking him out of my dreams, and now, it seemed like there was a bullseye on my back in real life.

There is a possessive undertone with him. The desire he holds is to overwhelm me, overtake me, to have me, and it makes my skin crawl. It feels impure and natural. Predatory, even, so the revelation of his return is haunting. I am still on a high from reaching a new plateau in my relationship with God and now I am puzzled.

I don't understand how we go from my high praise to me now feeling tested and stretched and fatigued from what is feeling like never-ending testing and stretching. I wonder, out loud, why so many obstacles to get what You told me was mine?! I feel pressure. Like this is significant and important. Like if I want what He said is mine, I must go through this. I say thanks but no thanks to lunch. If this must be done, I must be prepared.

The day before I'd listened to a Bishop Jakes sermon entitled 'You Can't Give Me What I Already Have.' The scripture was Matthew 4, Jesus' temptation in the wilderness. The teaching took the perspective that the test was about integrity. This immediately comes to mind, so I go back to it to study it. The teaching poses the question- **'how will you use your power?'** Moses was told by God to speak to the rock to produce water for Israel but frustrated by their murmuring he struck the rock instead, angering God. Moses misused the power that God had given him to vent his own bewilderment, robbing Israel's opportunity to see that He is God. This is the sin that God judges Moses for and ultimately keeps him from entering Canaan.

When Jesus is tempted, the devil is essentially asking that He use the power of God to satisfy His flesh- a misuse of the power of God. But Jesus, unlike Moses, refuses, maintaining His integrity and continues to His destiny.

I have a power in relationship to this love that I did not have when we were in love. It is what has drawn him to me in this season. It is the presence of God. If I am not careful, and allow past hurts, current circumstances or the hunger of my flesh to overpower me, I could, like Moses, use my power in error. I must stay sober and vigilant.

The sermon discussed the enemy's attempt to 'give' to Jesus the kingdoms of the world; the Bishop points out that the problem with this tactic is that the kingdoms of the world belong to God and Jesus- it's just a matter of time, so the devil cannot give to Jesus what is already His. This man, with every seemingly good thing he brings, cannot bring to me what is already promised to me. It's just a matter of time until I get what God told me I would have.

And then came my **AHA!** moment: this test is so much less about facing an obstacle between me and my promise. It's about my loyalty to the God with whom I am in relationship. Will I remain loyal to what He told me about what will be when I am standing face to face with what is? Will I remain true to His word or succumb to disbelief? Do I really believe Him? This is about me and Him. Do I know how to fight for Us?

Funny thing is- this thing me and the Lord got going on seems way too real, if you know what I mean? I feel like the dude from The Five Heartbeats – "every night I gotta fight to prove my love!" #itslevelstothis

Go Deeper

1. **Write about how your past is fighting you for your future.**

2. **Who's winning?**

EPILOGUE

I wrote these blog entries during the time that I walked most closely with my creator. I was more vulnerable than I'd been, and He required even more- that I publish my writings for public consumption. This was almost ten years ago. Since then, I have come undone and had to learn new ways of being woman and believer. Spirit reminded me that my experience wasn't just for me and that there was more still for me to do with what He'd orchestrated. And so, I hope that your reflections have unlocked places in your hearts that you were taught to ignore, and with many blessings, I wish you well as you learn who you are and to whom you belong.